FOCUS

Tips from 10 successful and wealthy people about Concentration, Productivity, and Learning

BY

MARK GRANT

Copyright © 2016 by Mark Grant. All rights reserved.

No part of this publication may be reproduced, distributed, or transmitted in any form or by any means, including photocopying, recording, or other electronic or mechanical methods, or by any information storage and retrieval system without the prior written permission of the publisher, except in the case of very brief quotations embodied in critical reviews and certain other noncommercial uses permitted by copyright law.

Table of Contents

- INTRODUCTION 4
- TONY ROBBINS 6
- MARK CUBAN 8
- WARREN BUFFETT 9
- STEVE JOBS 10
- RICHARD BRANSON 12
- OPRAH WINFREY 14
- JEFF BEZOS 15
- ARNOLD SCHWARZENEGGER 17
- ELON MUSK 19
- MARK ZUCKERBERG 21
- CONCLUSION 22
- NAVY SEALS SELF-DISCIPLINE 23
- ABOUT THE AUTHOR 46

INTRODUCTION

Each and every one of us works hard and strives to be successful in everything we do. However, success is not something that is a guaranteed return of hard work - many times, success evades most of us.

If you look at the successful people around you, you will realize, not only are they hard working individuals – they are also focused on their goal and passionate about the project at hand. Productivity, for them, is a significant element and it is directly proportionate to the success they achieve in life.

To improve productivity, it is important to improve your concentration and focus on your goals. Although, just saying we need to improve our concentration and focus doesn't cut the deal. The motivation to pull through a task and making it a success that comes from within is what sets you apart from others.

To inspire your journey, here is a compilation of a few tips from 10 of the world's most successful people. These tips will inspire you to give your absolute best while chasing down your goals. These tips will also help you increase your concentration, focus on your goals and improve your overall productivity.

The book has been designed for easy reading, and will inspire you to do your best in every field of life. It examines the ideologies of some of the most productive and resourceful people in the world, including the likes of Elon Musk, Oprah Winfrey, Mark Zuckerberg and much more.

So without any further delay, let us get started.

Tony Robbins

According to life coach Tony Robbins, many people suffer from being "wantrepreneurs". The term refers to those that wish to become an entrepreneur, but often neglect or forgo their dreams. Robbins believes that more and more people fall under the list of wantrepreneurs than that of entrepreneurs.

These mainly include those that live in fear and are not willing to take risks. However, continuing on the same route will not lead anywhere, and it is extremely important to go after one's dreams and ambitions. Failure is a part and parcel of life and should not stop one from chasing their dreams.

Many successful entrepreneurs such as Walt Disney and Oprah Winfrey have all failed at some point in their lives, but picked themselves up and went after their true desires.

Perseverance is key and so is hard work. The two go hand in hand and it is extremely important for an entrepreneur to focus on the end goal.

It will take some time for a wantrepreneur to become a successful entrepreneur and until such time, one has to commit themselves to whatever matters most, and do whatever it takes to follow and fulfill their dreams.

A real entrepreneur will not wait for things to fall into place, but will, instead, take initiative and set off on the right foot.

Finance is a big concern for many wantrepreneurs, but Robbins says that a good entrepreneur will bootstrap his current company, if it comes to that, to raise enough funds for the new one. A certain motivation and drive are what fuels a wantrepreneur to become a successful entrepreneur.

Mark Cuban

The owner of Dallas Mavericks, Mark Cuban, is one of the most successful billionaires in the world. Here are some tips that mark Cuban has shared to help people improve their productivity:

• "Work like there is someone working 24 hours a day to take it away from you"

One of the first and most important tip is to work really hard. This tip goes a long way in helping lazy people remain motivated and give it their best. It also puts the focus on the fact that there are hundreds out there who are vying for your job and it is important for you to excel at it.

• "It's not in the dreaming, it's in the doing"

It is obvious that everybody has dreams and ambitions that they wish to pursue. However, mere dreams don't help you attain rewards, it is important for you to fulfill them. You have to focus on the "do" more than on the "dreams".

• "Doesn't matter if the glass is half-empty or half-full. All that matters is that you are the one pouring the water"

This statement is just a reassurance of the fact that we are responsible for our own destiny. It is extremely important for us to take matters into our own hands, and try to mold our own destiny.

Warren Buffett

Multi-billionaire media mogul, Warren Buffet, is easily one of the best productivity gurus in the world. According to Buffet, the best way to be productive and go after one's goals is to follow a simple 3-step process:

Step 1: The first step is to write down the 25 most desired career goals that you wish to fulfill in your life. If you want to see quick results, then you can also write down the goals that you wish to attain within a week's time.

Step 2: Next, skim through your list and pick out 5 of the most important goals that you wish to attain.

Step 3: The last step is to work on the 5 important goals that were circled and IGNORE the 20 that were left out. Many people make the mistake of trying to simultaneously attain all their goals, which only results in them forgoing the important ones. It is, therefore, best to first pursue the important goals and go after the others, but only after the important ones have been successfully attained.

Buffet's advice to several multi-billionaires such as Bill Gates has proved to be extremely useful. For example, he asked Bill Gates to keep his schedule clear to be prepared to take on any impromptu task that comes his way. Similarly, you must prioritize your work in order to attain the best in life.

Steve Jobs

Apple Inc. mogul, the late, Steve Jobs, has served as an inspiration to millions of entrepreneurs around the world. Here are some tips from the guru himself:

• Focus on the Positives

No matter what the outcome of a venture is, it is extremely important for you to focus on the positives. Jobs always looked at the positive side of things, which helped him forge ahead.

• Finding the Right Partner

It is common knowledge that Jobs cofounded Apple Inc. with Steve Wozniak. The two worked together and shouldered equal responsibility. Similarly, everybody must make it a point to find the best partner to work with in order to increase productivity and attain success.

• Taking Risks

Taking risks was one of Jobs' strong points and he never backed away from taking a calculated risk. He developed the iPhone, despite knowing that it would make the iPod redundant. Similarly, you must forge ahead and take risks that will allow you to attain better results for your business.

- **DON'T REFRAIN FROM LEARNING FROM OTHERS**

It is important to draw inspiration from other people, especially those that you idolize. Jobs had worked for HP and ATARI and drew inspiration from the two. He looked at their business models, and designed one for apple, by building on the positives and avoiding the mistakes that these companies were making.

Richard Branson

It is no secret that Virgin mogul, Richard Branson, is a brilliant entrepreneur. Here are some productivity tips that he has shared over the years:

• Setting goals

Richard Branson constantly keeps a journal with him - where he jots down a "to-do list". This helps him keep track of everything that needs to be done within a day. You too must follow the same practice in order to ensure that you get everything done on time.

• Mental models

It is important for you to come up with mental models of your business plans. You don't have to write them down physically all the time. You have to create the models and compare it with whatever you are making. If the two match, then you can go ahead with it, but if there is a variation then you should fix the issues.

• Motivating yourself

You can achieve many of your desired goals by ensuring you remain motivated. It's all about working hard towards attaining the desires and taking requisite action. There is no point in setting out goals and not taking appropriate action.

You have to look at the goals every morning to see if you are on the right track.

• DELEGATION

It is important to delegate work to others; this is to ensure that you are free to take up any impromptu task. There is nothing wrong in seeking help and it is best to distribute work smartly. You should make a list of the tasks as well as a list of delegates and then assign work according to their strength.

OPRAH WINFREY

Oprah Winfrey's road to success has been filled with challenges, but she has managed to come out on top every single time. Oprah's biggest advice in terms of increasing productivity is to set deadlines.

Having reasonable deadlines helps in staving off procrastination, which can cause people to lag behind. She even sometimes sets herself false deadlines just to ensure that she gets the work done, on or before time.

A good trick is to write down all your tasks and then set a deadline for each. If you don't finish the task on time, then simply move on to the next one. Once you are done with the last task, you can go back and finish the first one.

It's a nice little way to finish all your tasks on time and not have to worry about leaving something out at the end of the day.

Jeff Bezos

Amazon founder, Jeff Bezos, is no stranger to productivity hacks and risks taking. After all, he was one of the first few in the world to move his offline business onto an online platform, which was on par with taking a major career risk.

Here are some tips from the guru himself:

• Remain frugal

If you wish to make the most of your business, then it is quite important for you to practice frugality. Bezos tries to control as much of the unnecessary expenditure as possible and ensures that the company is only spending on the necessary items. When you take away the pressure from your shoulders, then you automatically start to focus on the important tasks, which in turn increases your productivity.

• Think long term

It is paramount for you to think long term and not set just temporary goals. When Bezos started with amazon.com, the concept of eBooks was very new. But he knew that it would be big in the future and decided to start an Internet-oriented business. Similarly, you must identify the next big thing and pursue the same.

• Remain hungry

Don't be satisfied until you have achieved all your goals. And once you achieve them, you must set new ones and go after them. Doing so will help you aim higher and achieve bigger. Keep your competition in sight and make sure that you are one step ahead of them.

• SMART CHOICES

When Bezos decided to start amazon, he knew that books were a great bet. They are almost never returned by an unhappy customer and don't go bad or get damaged. Picking a product like that is sure to help you experience success.

Arnold Schwarzenegger

From starring in Hollywood movies to being the Governor of California, Arnold Schwarzenegger has done it all, and in great style. Here are some tips to take away from Arnold's book of success:

• Believe in yourself

Self-belief is extremely important and Arnold always believed in his own capabilities. You must stave off the naysayers and listen to yourself. If you think something will work for you then give it a try to see if you are correct. That's the only way in which you can attain your true desires.

• Keep distractions at bay

You have to try and avoid engaging in social media as much as possible, especially during your work hours. It has the potential to distract you and take your mind away from important tasks. It is fine to have a social media presence as long as it is not interfering with your productivity. Just like social media, you have to control unwanted emails. Identify the emails that are distracting you and block them to prevent them from bothering you in the future.

• Break the stereotype

Don't stick with the usual and try to think out of the box. Taking risks have always worked and it is best for you to try something outside of your comfort zone. Numerous individuals scrutinized Arnold's decision to become a movie star as he had a substantial massive body and a confusing accent. However, he went against the rules and became a very successful actor. People, once again, questioned his decision when he wished to be a politician, but he also managed to successfully govern.

Elon Musk

Tesla and SpaceX CEO, Elon Musk, is one of the most successful self-made billionaires in the world, and a role model to millions of young entrepreneurs worldwide.

Here are some productivity tips from the mogul himself:

• Nothing like hard work

Elon Musk said in an interview that he worked 100 hours a week for almost 15 years in order to set up his companies. Although, it is not everybody's cup of tea to match up to it, you can at least try to work 70 to 80 hours a week. Hard work always pays off regardless of the number and types of obstacles that come in the way.

• Be prepared

One productivity rule that Musk swears by is being prepared for anything. Musk is always prepared for a meeting or any other business related activity. Many Tesla employees have said that musk does not entertain anybody who comes in unprepared. It is important to make a positive contribution in order to stay on top.

• Seek criticism

According to Musk, it is important to have a fair share of criticism sent your way. Musk takes criticism and works on it to build a better product. That is the only way in which you can perfect something.

Mark Zuckerberg

Facebook founder, Mark Zuckerberg, has inspired many people with his, productivity and concentration hacks. Here are two of his most sought after advice:

• Wake up early

Mark Zuckerberg wakes up by 5am in the morning and gets straight to work. Waking up early gives you a better the chance to prepare for the day ahead. You don't have to wait until the last minute to get done with your day's work, hence you will have enough time to do more.

• Don't multi-task

Some people have the tendency to do many things at once. Although, this works well for some, it does not for a majority of the people and it is, therefore, important to tone down the multi-tasking to focus on a single task at a time.

Conclusion

With that, we have come to the end of this book. I hope the tips shared by these established individuals would help you carve your own path to success. I am sure you noticed that these individuals didn't do anything out of the box, they are just focused on doing the right thing.

Now that you have learned their secret to success, it is now time to simulate their values and make them your own. Thank you for your time you spent reading this book. I appreciate it.

Navy Seals
Self-Discipline

Training and Self-Discipline to Become Tough Like A Navy SEAL

INTRODUCTION

You might have heard about Navy SEALs, but do you know everything about what they do? A quick background will help you get a better understanding.

Navy SEALS are one of the most elite group of fighters in the world, but there is so much more to being a SEAL than fighting. They do operate in a world that's far different from our own, but their training can prove to be a useful weapon in your arsenal for achieving success.

QUICK BACKGROUND

In the year 1962, under the orders of President Kennedy, the United States Navy had established a special sea, air, and land team known as Navy SEALS. The Navy SEALS are considered to be an elite group of specialists who are trained to engage in unconventional combat. High-impact missions that require stealth—which cannot be carried out by large forces like tanks and submarines—are carried out by the SEALs. For all the operations that either start or end in water bodies like swamps, oceans, coastlines, and so on, the go-to team of specialists for Navy, Air Force, and even Army Special Forces would be the SEALs. Though the Navy SEALs belong to the naval unit of United States, they are trained to engage in missions on all types of terrains and extreme climatic conditions as well.

This book contains proven steps and strategies on how to train yourself mentally, physically, and emotionally like a Navy SEAL to achieve your goals. Well, it is likely that you won't be on par with the well-trained SEALs but you can definitely make use of their principles in your day-to-day life.

Chapter One: Training Regimen of Navy SEALs

Mind Over Matter

The human body is made up of many different organs, but the brain is considered to be the most powerful of all. You wouldn't be able to perform even the simplest of functions—like moving your muscles—if your brain wasn't functioning. You might have heard stories of heroism performed by men on battlefields that saved not just their lives but also of those around them. They wouldn't have been able to do so if they weren't mentally strong. Navy SEALs are trained in such a manner that their brain can override their physical pain and push them to function in a manner that would usually seem impossible. Mental preparation is the key to unlocking your true potential.

The brain is a muscle, and you will be able to train it by engaging in some mental exercises. You can do these mental exercises any time and place. You can exercise your mind to unlock your potential by engaging your mind in the following exercises.

Battle-proofing will help you to condition your mind to react in hostile situations and emergencies, by developing mental strength for managing a crisis. This can be done by visualizing intense fights. When you start battle-proofing your brain, it will start believing that you have experienced all that you have imagined. Whenever a similar situation comes up, you will be able to take quick action.

You will need to create your own "triggers." A trigger is something that can help you ignite the qualities that are necessary for not just your survival but for your personal growth as well. Your trigger could be a memory, a phrase, or an experience that can move your mind and soul towards achieving your goals.

You should train your mind to get out of situations that would stress you out unnecessarily and this will help you to gain control over a situation.

Navy SEALs are trained not to act on the first impulse that pops into their mind, but to consider all the possible ways of acting in a critical situation. You will be able to do this only when you can reign in your thoughts and control your mind.

When you are truly aware of your insecurities and true motivations, you will be able to avoid making the same mistakes again and can move forward. Understanding the purpose behind your job, whether you are a Navy SEAL or not, will help you excel. Learn to make yourself as happy as you can be in any given situation and don't do anything halfheartedly.

Have faith in yourself, surround yourself with positive company, always focus on the present, and don't live in your past or future. Lastly, learn to control your breathing. Navy SEALs are tough men, not just because of their bodies but because of their minds as well.

Various Stages of Training

Warfare preparatory school

The training curriculum for becoming a Navy SEAL starts at the Naval Special Warfare Preparatory School referred to as NSW Prep, in Great Lakes, Illinois, and lasts for 8 weeks. The aim of NSW Prep is to prepare the SEAL candidates to endure the grueling physical trials of BUD/S. NSW Prep ends with a PST that you must pass if you want to become a SEAL. It begins with a Physical Screening Test and ends with a grueling PST that includes a 1,000 yard swim to be completed in or under 20 minutes, 60 curl-ups in 2 minutes, 70 push-ups in 2 minutes, 10 pull-ups in 2 minutes, and a four mile run with shoes and pants that needs to be completed within 31 minutes.

BUD/S Training – 3 phases

BUD/S stands for Basic Underwater Demolition/SEAL Training, and this helps to develop the physical and mental strength of the candidates who want to become Navy SEALs. BUD/S lasts for 7 months and has different phases that test the physical, emotional, mental strength, and also leadership skills of the candidates. BUD/S has a three-week orientation, followed by the three phases mentioned below.

Indoctrination:

This lasts for three weeks, and introduces the candidates to the BUD/S lifestyle at Coronado: the Naval Special Warfare Center. The INDOC is designed to help prepare the candidates for the training they have to undergo in the three phases.

Phase 1: The first phase lasts for seven weeks and it assesses the SEAL candidates in different areas of physical conditioning: proficiency in water, teamwork skills, and mental strength. Physical conditioning includes swimming, running, and calisthenics, and the course grows harder every week. The first two weeks of this training prepares them for the third week, also referred to as "hell week". The candidate has to take part in five and a half days of strenuous training with maybe 4 hours of sleep for the entire week, and the training can exceed 20 hours a day. After the "hell week," the remaining 4 weeks are spent learning different methods of creating hydrographic charts and conducting various hydrographic surveys.

Phase 2: This lasts for 7 weeks and is the diving phase, aimed at training and developing the SEAL candidates' skills as combat swimmers. The physical training becomes more intensive and focuses on combat scuba. It focuses on open as well as closed circuit scuba. Basic medical training and dive medicine skills training is given. This phase helps make sure that the applicants are capable of making use of swimming and diving techniques as transportation from their basic launch points. If a candidate wants to complete the second phase, they would have to showcase an extreme level of comfort and ability to perform in stressful and tough circumstances.

Phase 3: This lasts for 7 weeks and trains the candidates in land warfare like the usage of basic weapons, land navigation, demolitions, patrolling, rappelling, and small unit tactics. There is a lot of classroom work that teaches them to read maps, use compass, and to collect and process information for completing their mission. These skills allow the candidates to become more comfortable while out in the field.

For the last three and a half weeks of the training, the class is taken offshore to San Clemente Island. Here they get to practice all the skills that they have acquired in the third phase. The training and work becomes more intensive in order to mirror the work they get in field. This is the most intensive part of training, because the training goes on for all seven days of the week with minimal sleep, while handling dangerous explosives and ammunition. Also, the punishments for mistakes at this stage of training are extremely harsh.

Parachute Jump School:

After the completion of BUD/S the SEAL candidates proceed to San Diego, California to learn static and free fall training at Tactical Air Operations. This is a 3-week program that is conducted by highly trained and qualified instructors and it is designed to help transform the SEAL candidates into competent free fall jumpers within a short duration of time. At the end of the training they should be able to complete night descents in all their combat equipment from an altitude of at least 9500 feet.

Graduation

The SEALs training concludes with the BUD/S class graduation, where the candidates who managed to survive the grueling training stand proud in their Navy uniform and receive the pins with the Trident insignia, the symbol of becoming an official Navy SEAL. The achievements of the new SEAL recruits are recognized in the presence of various senior SEAL leaders, Senior advisors of Naval Special Warfare groups, Naval Commanding Officers, other SEAL teams, and family members.

Post-graduation training

The SEAL training doesn't end with becoming a part of the SEALs. Even after graduation, they continue to be put through extensive training before they are sent out into the field on missions. The BUD/S was just a qualifying training program and it is only after continuous training will they be qualified as SEALs officially. Once the recruits have been assigned to a particular SEAL Team, then their troop training begins. This is pre-deployment training, it can last from 12-18 months, and is divided into three phases that include: individuality specialty training, unit level training, and task group level training.

The training that they go through is extremely tough and testing on the body, mind, and spirit. Going through it might not be possible for all of us, but we can definitely implement a few of their practices in our daily life for becoming more successful.

WHAT IS NAVY SEAL SELF-DISCIPLINE AND WHY SHOULD YOU LEARN FROM THEM?

The reason for this is simply, training like a Navy SEAL will make you more confident in yourself. When you are mentally, physically, and emotionally strong, you will never feel incapable of achieving something that you want. You needn't be a Navy SEAL in order to win, you just need to adopt a few of their principles.

Physical fitness

Being physically fit and in shape does go a long way when it comes to boosting your self-confidence. This might sound vain, or even superficial, but it's the truth. Training the way that SEALs do will definitely help you achieve great physical strength and fitness.

Mental Toughness

Most of the battles that we face in our life are mental or emotional. The SEALs are considered to be amongst the world's physically superior specimens, but their mental conditioning is just as important as their physical superiority. Most of the time, it's mental trauma that cripples them. Only those who are mentally and emotionally fit can survive being a SEAL. This will also make you a confident person.

Situational Awareness

Being aware of yourself and the situation you are in can help a great deal when you are on the path towards achieving your goals. You shouldn't have any illusions about who you are and what you are doing. Always be sensitive to your surroundings and this will help you figure out exits and different strategies for getting yourself where you want to be.

Quick Action

Being able to take quick action in a situation of crisis is extremely important for the SEALs. In the situations they usually find themselves in, even a small mistake or delay can prove to be life threatening—not just for themselves, but for those around them as well. You can condition your mind to act in a certain manner in a specific situation and when the time comes, your mind will automatically do what it has been programmed to do instead of wasting precious time figuring out a course of action.

Chapter Two: How To Develop Self Discipline the SEAL Way: Part I

Through Improving Physical Fitness

Due to the extremely demanding situations they have to face, Navy SEALs always have to stay in their finest physical shape if they want to carry out their missions successfully. Navy SEALs need to be in good cardiovascular shape, nimble, strong, and quick. Cardio and calisthenics are the most important aspects of their physical fitness programs.

Cardio

Navy SEALs usually have to disembark really far from shores in order to approach the enemy territory as stealthily as possible. At times they need to swim great distances with their weapons and gear on. Well, if you swim, you might realize that swimming in a pool for 10 laps can drain you completely, but if you have to swim with all the added weight of your weapons, that's really tough. You needn't swim 1 kilometer in the open sea or run 1.5 miles under 11 minutes while wearing your army boots, but doing cardio regularly will help you to stay in great shape. Cardio helps to increase your heart rate and improves the delivery of oxygen to the various muscles in the body to burn out all the fat. The most practical way of doing cardio is running. You just need a pair of good running shoes and you are set. The only limitation that you will have to overcome is your mind. Swimming, cycling, and even jogging are good forms of cardio.

Calisthenics

Bodyweight exercises are an extremely important part of fitness regimes, and calisthenics helps you to stay in shape without building any excess muscle. When it comes to combat, functional strength is the most important factor that you should take into consideration. Lifting strength and functional strength are extremely different. For example, scaling a wall requires functional strength and not lifting strength—a gymnast would be able to scale a wall easily when compared to a bodybuilder who can pull down 400 pounds! Grip push-ups, pull-ups, bodyweight back extensions, squats, lunges, jumping squats, sit-ups, crunches, planks, burpees, trunk twists, and so on are good calisthenics exercises. You can start out by working three times a week and increase it to four to five times a week. Make sure that you are working out all the muscle groups and not overdoing it.

Yoga

Yoga is extremely good for developing mental and physical strength. Your mind will become more alert and you will feel yourself getting stronger spiritually as well. There are different yoga poses that you can do depending upon the part of the body that you want to work on. Breathing exercises will help you to calm your mind, and ensure the optimum supply of oxygen to various parts of your body for their better functioning. Anulom vilom, kapalbhati and Bhrastrika pranayama will help you regulate your breathing. Yoga poses like tree pose, cobra pose, triangle pose, shoulder stand pose, plough pose, bow pose, fish pose, forward bend, downward dog, and child's pose will help in developing core strength.

Running

Running is an important part of Navy SEAL training, and you will need to concentrate on form and effort to improve your running potential. If you want to build your stamina, then long slow distance would be the most ideal style to start with. Agility is extremely important for SEALs because they need to traverse great distances on foot and run around a lot while carrying all their ammunition and gear. Running at a consistent, moderate pace for long distance will improve your stamina greatly. Continuous high intensity running is tough, but it will help you achieve and maintain a great speed for a longer duration of time. You can also adopt high intensity exercises combined with short intervals between them, like cross fit.

THROUGH IMPROVING NUTRITION

Aside from performing all the rigorous activities and exercises that the SEALs have to, they also need to have nutritious food daily. When it comes to physical health as well as fitness, nutrition plays a very important role. You might have seen people who regularly and religiously work out at the gym and still look like the Michelin Man. This is because of their poor diet that's full of sugar and fats.

Diet plan for the whole day

Navy SEALs have a very demanding job and for them, having nutritional meals is very important to keep performing well. Navy SEALs follow NOFFS (Navy Operational Fitness and Fueling Series) for maintaining optimal nutrition. The NOFFS limits the consumption of processed foods and encourages the consumption of whole foods that are good for the body. High carbohydrate and protein consumption along with fiber is extremely important for SEALs, for maintaining their strength and stamina.

For good metabolism, SEALs eat small and frequent meals. They eat about 4 to 6 meals every day with a gap of at least two hours between each meal. This prevents binge eating and helps burn calories as well. This is a good way of eating, not just for the SEALs, but for everyone in general.

Consuming carbohydrates the size of your fist, proteins the size of your palm, dietary fats the size of tip of your thumb would be sufficient for a normal person.

A Navy SEAL would have his first meal before working out at 6:00 a.m., and it would include something that has a little fat content to keep them going, like an omelet made of egg whites and 2 slices of wheat toast. Eat as many grains as possible, but avoid white bread and pasta.

The second meal would be at 9:00 a.m. after working out and consumption of carbs is permitted now. This will help in the transportation of insulin throughout your body after the workout. 2 bananas with a glass of milk with reduced fat content, or oatmeal with raisins and skim milk is a good option as well. You can always add a fruit if you are hungry.

The third meal would be around 12:00 p.m., and this would be your lunch. Avoid oily and fried items as well as the stuff that you find in the vending machines. You can consider having a whole wheat wrap or sandwich with turkey in it and as many vegetables as you like except those that are high in carbs. A few baked potato chips would be good, and broccoli to maintain your fiber intake. Also, you can have a fruit or some yogurt for desert.

At 3:00 p.m. you can have your fourth meal that can consists of a can of tuna or some egg whites on a whole wheat bagel, or a slice of bread. Something light to keep your energy levels up and your hunger in check would be a good idea. Low fat yogurt and vegetables would be good too.

The fifth meal should be consumed around 5:00 p.m. and you can include something really light, because you would consume your dinner in a few hours. Have a small salad or a snack like wheat crackers to nibble on. A glass of fruit juice, protein shake, or even coconut water would make you feel energized. But avoid fat at all cost; you wouldn't want to regain all the fat that you burnt while working out.

The sixth meal for the day is dinner; have it at around 6:30 p.m. Include multigrain pasta or anything else that gives you some carbs and proteins, a little bit of bread, and some protein in the form of chicken or turkey breast, fish, or a really lean stake. Add in as many vegetables as you want and some greens to make a complete and healthy meal. Give yourself at least two to three hours before heading to bed so that your stomach can digest all that you have consumed.

Healthy Eating – Quick Tips

Here are some tips that you can keep in mind if you want to eat healthy every day, just like Navy SEALs:

• You can consume 5 to 6 meals every day that are spaced out with an interval of at least three hours between each meal. Consume small meals and don't binge.

• Don't skip your meals and make sure your diet is rich in protein, some complex carbs, and a little bit of fat as well, but not processed sugar. Eat till you feel full, but don't stuff yourself.

• Remember to exercise every day; don't skip this step. You needn't undergo the rigorous physical regimen followed by SEALs, but do exercise.

• Drink lots of water and keep yourself hydrated throughout the day. Drink some water before every meal and also after every meal. Keep a few healthy snacks on hand whenever hunger and cravings creep in.

• You should always chew your food well and don't swallow it without chewing. Don't starve yourself; eat regularly if you are having small meals.

Chapter Three: How To Develop Self Discipline the SEAL Way – Part II

Through Overcoming Fear

Fear can be crippling. If you overcome your fear you will be able to think clearly and you will be able to tackle the problem at hand in a better manner. But if you let your fear get a hold of you, then the outcome won't be positive. SEALs are trained in such a manner that their brains wouldn't let fear creep in. If you can also train your mind in a similar manner you will be able to discipline yourself and focus on your goals.

Habituation

The reason why SEALs are fearless when compared to other human beings is because of their training, and a psychological technique that is referred to as habituation. This is the process of exposing a person to things or situations that he or she is scared of, repeatedly. Repeated exposure will help the person to overcome their fears, because they start getting used to them and will be immune to it. This is a case of mind over matter. One of the primary weapons of the modern army are the minds of people who comprise it. For becoming a successful Navy SEAL you not only need to be physically fit but also mentally strong.

Setting Goals

Setting short-term and very specific goals will help you perform better. Set small goals that you know you will be able to accomplish with a little extra effort. When you complete or achieve a goal, it will fill you with a sense of accomplishment that will help you in not only performing better, but it will also improve your confidence and boot your morale. According to studies conducted by neuroscientists, the trainees who set short-term goals managed to have a higher rate of success than those who didn't. This technique can be used by anyone, not just the SEALs. Don't bother yourself with what might happen after you have completed the task. Instead, simply focus on the task at hand.

Visualization

This is a technique that is frequently used by sportsmen and even musicians when they want to improve their skills. Whenever they take a break, they visualize themselves as either performing or playing a piece of music perfectly, or swinging their bat really well. Practicing mental visualizations is as important as performing the task itself. During the training sessions, the SEALs have to don their scuba gear and perform emergency drills while underwater. All the while they might keep getting harassed by their instructor who would make the drill tougher by cutting off their oxygen supply or tying up the scuba pipes. In such a situation, they need to keep their calm and practice visualization, because this helps the brain to automatically switch to the mode where it does everything for achieving the goal on hand without much trouble. This is an incredible motivational technique that will definitely help in performing better. Your mind will want to experience the joy it experiences when you visualized the completion of the task, and this will push you to achieve the goal that was set.

Positive Self Talk

Did you know that you talk to yourself at a rate of anywhere between 800 to 1,600 words per minute? That's a lot, isn't it? Imagine if you engage in a negative conversation with yourself for 5 minutes, you will have said around 4,000 negative words to yourself. Well, that doesn't sound fair to you. Navy SEALs are taught simple techniques of self-hypnotism that help them overcome all of the negative thoughts, and instead helps them to focus their energy on positive thoughts and actions. This would act as a motivational factor and help them to move along when the going gets tough.

THROUGH DEVELOPING SITUATIONAL AWARENESS

Situational awareness is of great importance, especially for the Navy SEALs because they are often in such risky situations where one wrong move might prove to be fatal for themselves and all those around them. You can also improve your self-discipline by working on your situational awareness by doing the following.

Arousal Control

Being able to control your state of mind is a very important factor for the Navy SEALs. There are different knee-jerk reactions that are hardwired into our system and fine-tuning them can be quite difficult. For instance, sweaty palms and shaky hands are common symptoms of being scared or nervous. These are natural bodily reactions that are designed for helping you stay out of trouble. This is something that cannot be controlled, and is caused by strong hormones, like adrenaline and cortisol. Controlling the secretion of these hormones is also hard when you are stressed or scared. Navy SEALs are required to perform in extremely demanding circumstances and it is extremely important for them to control these knee-jerk reactions. Practicing deep breathing helps to control your reactions and clear your mind.

Waiting Patiently

Patience might not come easily, but it is a very important trait if you are a SEAL. You will need to be patient and you shouldn't rush anything without thinking things through. Your first thought or impulse might not always be right. There might be alternative ways of doing a single task; go through the possible list very patiently without rushing. This will help you in making the best decision. Impatience will just push you to make rash decisions that could harm you and all those around you. Learn to be patient and you can start to discipline your mind.

Controlling Breathing

Taking deep breaths is also a very effective relaxation technique and it also helps you to think clearly so that you don't make a hurried decision that can be potentially damaging. Whenever you feel that you are panicking, take a few deep breaths and close your eyes. This will help you to calm your mind so that you can think clearly once again without the veil of panic clouding your vision. A Navy SEAL needs to learn to think clearly even in situations of distress, and this skill will definitely come in handy.

Close Observation

Observational skills are very important, and developing them is no easy task. Whether you are a civilian or not, it takes a long time to develop these skills. For SEALs it is extremely important to develop their observational skills because it would help them in their survival! It becomes really difficult to develop this skill when you are a civilian, but it can be done by playing a simple game. The awareness game is something that will help you to develop your observational skills easily. Whenever you are outside, notice little things about those around you and make a mental note of what you observe. When you go home, recollect what you observed and compare the same with what others observed. In a life-threatening situation, like when you are stuck in fire, noticing and remembering a fire exit will definitely come in handy.

Self-discipline is important in every aspect of life, regardless of whether or not you are a Navy SEAL. It helps to control your impulses and to achieve the goals that you have set for yourself by taking the right course of action. When your mind is disciplined, there is nothing you cannot achieve.

Conclusion

Thank you again for downloading this book!

I hope it was able to help you to understand the qualities that make Navy SEALs tough, and that you can also start training like them: physically, mentally, emotionally, and also nutritionally to become more confident. You might not become as tough as an actual Navy SEAL, but you can definitely achieve your goals by making use of the same principles.

The next step is to apply whatever you have learned in your life, as soon as possible. This will definitely help you change your life positively. Don't rush through these things. Take your time and implement these things slowly.

Thank you and good luck.

About the Author

Hi, I'm Mark and here's a little about me:

I'm an entrepreneur, internet marketer, author, life coach, professional speaker, fitness enthusiast, and world traveler. I feel extremely blessed for the life that I live.

I bring 7 years of niche expertise in self-help and personal development. I'm a business management graduate and I like to study people who appear to be unbeatable against all oddities or challenges of life. I seek answers for failures, lack of growth and thus I want to help people reinvent themselves. I believe: Each and every person is the sole controller of his/her life. If you do not take an utmost care of your life, no one else will.

ONE LAST THING...

If you enjoyed this book or found it useful I'd be very grateful if you'd post a short review on Amazon. Your support really does make a difference and I read all the reviews personally so I can get your feedback and make this book even better.

Thanks again for your support!

www.ingramcontent.com/pod-product-compliance
Lightning Source LLC
Chambersburg PA
CBHW070416190526
45169CB00003B/1281